In God We Trust

Iris Romeo

ISBN: 978-1-934246-99-3
Library of Congress: 2007943694
Printed in the U.S.A.
Printed January, 2008

DEDICATED TO

Justine Alonzo
(Ann Marie's lifelong friend)

Michelle Richardson
(Her friend through life)

Francine DeVivo Bennett
(Her cousin/soulmate)

ACKNOWLEDGEMENTS

Acknowledgement is made for use
of the following copyrighted material:

The song "By Heart" on page *ix*,
co-written by Jim Brickman and Hollye Leven
and published by Brickman Arrangement (SESAC)
and Swimmer Music (SESAC) and Hollye Peno Music
and Polygram Music Publishing (BMI).

CONTENTS

CONTENTS

Friends of Iris and Orlando

Another Family's Pain

SO MANY DIMES

So many dimes, so many dimes!
I have found so many dimes!

The reason my friends, I do not know,
Of why a dime, I found in the snow!!

A rug just cleaned, a floor just shined,
And there again, one more dime!!!!!

The car has been shined, vacuumed and waxed,
But still, a lone dime lies in the back!

I used to question, I used to wonder,
Of how the dime got buried way under.

It matters no more, I just accept
The fact that "Annie: is with us yet!!

She drops me a dime where 'ere I go,
To say, "I'm okay, please let my parents know!"

I am the possessor of forty or more,
In a small box is where they are stored!

I hope in my life, there will be more dimes to come.
I would feel so empty if they were all done!!

So Annie please, keep thinking of me,
Just drop me more dimes, They make me happy!

Written by Kathy Kovzelove

This is just a little poem that came to me today after Iris left!! She had stopped over for a cup of coffee and Happy New Year greeting!!!!! It just amazes me how a bond of forty or so years is as strong today as the first day it was formed!!!

FOREWORD

Starting this book is one of the hardest things I have ever done in my life. I have tried to come up with all kinds of excuses for not writing it, but did not succeed. The events that led up to the writing of the book have affected many people's lives. I would like to thank Mary Alonzo and Frank Levanti for their help in taking this idea and making it into a reality. This book is a tribute to Ann Marie and to all the people who have contributed their stories.

ANN MARIE ROMEO
July 14, 1969 - November 12, 1990

By Heart
Co-Written by Jim Brickman and Hollye Leven

Hold me close, baby please
Tell me anything, but that you're going to leave
As I kiss this fallen tear,
I promise you I will be here.

Till the stars fall from the sky
Till I find a reason why
And darling, as the years go by
Till there's no more tears left to cry
Till the angels close my eyes
And even if we're worlds apart
I'll find my way back to you,
By Heart.

When you go I'll start to cry
I won't ever let this moment stop
Time is stealing you from me
But it can never take this memory.

Till the stars fall from the sky
Till I find the reason why
And darling, as the years go by
Till there's no more tears left to cry
Till the angels close my eyes
And even if we're worlds apart
I'll find my way back to you,
By Heart.

In Appreciation

As I mentioned in the forward, I had a difficult time getting this project started. At the end of summer in August of 1997, I went to North Carolina to help my son, Carmen and daughter-in-law, Louise move into their new home. It was during this time that Louise would be playing the music of Jim Brickman. They had taken Orlando and I earlier that year to see him in concert at the Bushnell in Hartford, CT. It was because of his music that I was finally inspired to start writing. The song, By Heart, from his CD, By Heart, explains exactly how I feel through the words and music.

With much gratitude,

Iris

INTRODUCTION

My daughter, Ann Marie, died on November 12, 1990, at approximately nine o'clock in the morning, as a result of a traffic accident while returning home from a college seminar. Her passing has forever changed the lives of everyone who knew her. We all look at things differently now. A beautiful sunset, an autumn day, wild flowers in a field, objects of beauty, all the things that we take for granted in our daily lives are things that she will never see again. Her memory will always be a part of us all. It is because of her passing and memory that this book is being written.

In 1964, I married Orlando Romeo, and soon after, we started our family. We had four children who were born into a loving family and community of friends. All the years that our children were growing up were filled with the normal ups and downs that most families experience.

Our children, Carmen, Christine, Ann Marie, and Angela all had wonderful friends throughout their growing years who impacted their lives and grew with them into wonderful, mature and loving human beings.

Ann Marie met Justine Alonzo when she was in kindergarten. I could remember her coming home asking if she could play with her. Because I had two older children and one younger, I did not initiate their getting together. Justine's mom called one day to introduce herself and to see if our children could play together after school. This was the beginning of a lifelong friendship for all of us. When the girls started third grade, they joined the local Girls' Club. The Club was located in the downtown area of our city, and was the girls' first adventure away from the neighborhood. Mary, Justine's mom, insisted that whenever her daughters went anywhere, they must carry a dime for a phone call in case of an emergency. We two mothers would car pool and felt comfortable knowing our daughters could call us if there were a problem. From that day on, Ann Marie would always carry a dime with her wherever she went. She carried this tradition with her throughout grammar school, high school and college.

When Ann Marie started at Holy Cross High School as a freshman, she met her dear friend, Michelle. We were all in line on "book day" and the two girls struck up a conversation. They remained dear friends from that day on. Even though both girls went to different colleges, they were always in constant touch with one another.

During all of Ann's life, she had been blessed with people who loved her so deeply that she thrived and flourished because of them. Justine and Michelle remained friends throughout her life. One other soulmate in her life was her cousin, Francine, who lived in New York. They were born nine months apart and shared an inseparable relationship from infancy through adulthood.

On November 12, 1990, at 3:00 a.m., Orlando and I received the phone call that no parent ever wants to get. We were told that Ann Marie was injured in an automobile accident in Scranton, Pennsylvania, and was in very serious condition. We arrived at the hospital four hours later. We were able to be with Ann Marie for another two hours before she passed away. During these hours, two of our dear friends left Waterbury to meet us at the hospital and to later drive us home. We were given her personal effects that day by a hospital social worker. When we arrived home, I put her clothes in her room. Days later, I remember giving her leather jacket to Michelle. Not to our surprise, there was a dime still in the jacket pocket.

It was during this time that Michelle told me she had sketched a drawing in her college art appreciation class. The drawing assignment had to relate to some part of the human anatomy. The separation of the girls, after a summer of being together, was so difficult that Michelle decided to draw an outstretched hand with a dime in the palm. This reminded her of Ann Marie and all the dimes she had handed out to everyone in the past. Michelle's instructor thought she had done a great job and displayed the sketch in an exhibition.

During the two weeks that followed Ann Marie's funeral, our home was filled with many friends and family members who helped write out thank you responses for all the donations of food, flowers, memorials and mass cards received during this time of our grief. By the time two weeks had passed, we had written out eight hundred fifty thank you cards.

It was at the end of this time, on a Wednesday night, that Orlando and I received a call from Michelle. I'll never forget answering the phone at 11:50 PM. The call jolted me, but not as bad as the reason for her call. Michelle was crying, and it took some time for her to tell us what happened. She told us that earlier that evening, she was in her apartment and found a dime. She assumed it was a coincidence, but when she found a second dime a while later, she really fell apart. She thought maybe her roommate or friends had put the dimes in the room to try to comfort her. When confronted, they swore that they would never do anything like that to her. They convinced Michelle that she should go out for a while. They all went to a local restaurant for a drink. Michelle was having a miserable time and excused herself to use the rest room. When she came back to the bar and sat down, there was a dime under her elbow.

We realized how affected she was by all of this. She was looking for some answers from us as to why this could happen. My response to her was to just accept and not question it. I told her that there were no answers to some things in life and that she should embrace the experience for whatever it meant. Orlando and I both tried to sleep knowing how hard this was on everyone.

Three days later, our housekeeper and friend, Charlie, had cleaned our house from top to bottom while we tried to pick up our lives and return to some kind of normalcy. It was after Charlie left when Mary came to visit and I told her what had happened with Michelle that Wednesday evening. I had also shared this story with some of my close relatives and friends during the week. When Mary left, I received a phone call and as I was hanging up, looked into the dining room and saw something shiny on the floor under the glass tea cart. I could remember my heart racing before I was able to clearly see what it was. I instinctively knew it was a dime. This dime was special because it was a Canadian dime with the woman's head, unlike the American dime with a man's head. I got very emotional finding it and called Michelle immediately to let her know what had happened. I was still in an emotional state when Orlando came home at 4:10 P.M. He arrived home from his first Saturday back to work. I showed him the dime on the dining room table, he picked it up and held it while we both cried. We both headed to the bedroom to get ready for the five o'clock mass. As we entered the bedroom, the phone rang. I don't remember who it was, but I know I was emotional throughout the call. As I hung up and started down to the other end of the bed, I looked down and there on the carpet was a shiny, new Canadian dime. I'm the type of person who has always tried not to get hysterical, but I started yelling at Orlando. "There can't be two dimes the same in this house! You must have put the one that was on the dining room table in your pocket and dropped it as you walked into the bedroom. It must have fallen when you reached into your pocket as you always do. Go out there and you will see that there isn't another dime on the table. It's impossible!!!!" We both walked out and sure enough, there on the table, was the original dime.

Inside of four days, Michelle, Orlando and I had found five dimes. I knew that no sound reasonable explanation could be found, so I accepted everything that had happened with a feeling that it was greater than we were. Let be what will be. From that day on, until the writing of this book, there have been so many dimes found by so many of our dear friends and family, that none of us question where, why or how. We put our trust in God and accept. Those who have found dimes have written the following stories. Some of us have found many dimes over these past seven years, but the following stories are most poignant to the hearts of the finders.

*The following stories are from those
to whom this book is dedicated...*

Justine

I have tried to explain to friends the significance dimes now hold for me. Outside of my family, my friend Lori is really the only other person who innately understands this and believes that these events are happening for a reason. Belief provides solace and warmth in a world where people prefer to ignore or dismiss what they do not truly understand. There have been many dimes found since Ann Marie died and not one has failed to stir my love for her and to cause me to feel her presence very near to me.

The most moving dime-finding experience for me occurred in the winter of 1997. I had to travel to Troy, Michigan on business that could not be rescheduled, When I had visited the client toward the end of 1996, we joked that we needed to pray for tame weather for our January meeting. As I packed my bag that morning, the weather was not cooperating. I had to go to the office before heading to the airport. As is usual in my line of work, the phone would not stop ringing, the people on the other end announcing problems, which required my immediate attention, and the fax machine kept supplying me with another reason to delay my journey to the airport.

Finally, the assistant for our group insisted that I hang up the phone and leave for my trip. I literally dragged my feet out of the building. Then, as I unlocked my car door, there was not one, but two dimes neatly lying on the ground. I do not remember the dimes being on the ground when I got out of the car earlier that morning. More importantly, finding two dimes instantly instilled in me an overall feeling of calmness and well-being. Suddenly, I knew that I was going to get to Troy, regardless of the weather.

At the meeting, as I joked with the client about how our prayers regarding the weather were not heard, I knew I was not being completely truthful. My prayers were heard. The answer seemed to be that I needed to face life, do what I needed to do, but that Ann Marie would be there with me, just to make sure I did it.

Michelle

I have so many thoughts and memories of Ann, where do I begin? This may sound selfish, but most of my memories and thoughts I can't share because they are between Ann and myself. The most important story I have you already know about. It is the one about the very first dime found in the leather jacket. It was very symbolic to me that the only thing in the snapped pocket of the jacket she wore to her death was a dime. This was the one she used to call her parents with the night of the accident. Ann always called her parents when she was going to be late or had a change of plans, thus she always carried a dime.

I have found so many dimes since that first one, that I do not often stop to think about it, I only stop and smile. So trying to write a story about finding dimes is difficult for me. Which ones should I tell you about? I found two together beneath the car door the night before I graduated from college and another two under my barstool later that evening. What about the one that fell to the ground as I walked into the room, or the one after vacuuming, or under my foot in the back seat of a car, or on the couch where I sit, or as I walk into a room before a stressful situation? These aren't like getting a dime mixed in with change back from a cashier, these are unique experiences! There are many more where those came from. For me, it is not the finding of a dime, but the feeling I get that matters. It is this feeling that will usually make my day. I could be very down and out, or having a wonderful time with friends. Either way, finding a dime fills my heart with love and reminds me of the wonderful friend I once had in Ann. My friend continues to watch over me in spirit even though she can not be here in body and mind. This is what the dimes mean to me.

Shall I mention the strange coincidences that also let me know Ann is with me? Like when I feel a brush of wind, a presence of sorts, or hearing the whispering of my name, or the feeling as if I'm being followed, led, pushed or pulled? One example would be the time when I was in a clothing store in Boston where I felt this presence upon entering. I didn't take it seriously until items started falling off the racks ahead and behind me several times. I finally had to leave the store so people wouldn't think I was possessed. It would be hard for anyone to understand that it was my invisible friend. In that respect, she still makes me laugh. Another time when I was in graduate school, our friend Jen and I were in our room talking. As we mentioned Ann's name, the helium balloon which was at the ceiling floated down and landed between us, deciding at that moment to run out of air.

One of the things that all of us friends always did was to beep twice whenever we would leave one another's house, sort of like an extended, "Bye, see you soon." I have continued this habit whenever I leave Ann's grave site. That information will be needed for this next story. Another night, while still in graduate school, about 3:00 AM, I awoke to a knocking, which turned out to be non-existent to everyone else in the house. When I opened my eyes, I felt this presence and saw a shadow in the corner, more like an angelic light. At first I was startled (because for years I had been dreaming of Ann but she never spoke to me until this time) but then felt very calm and relaxed.. At that moment I realized how quiet and peaceful my house and surroundings were. Not a sound was to be heard until a car drove by and beeped twice! Is that only a coincidence? Maybe, but it gives me comfort, as does turning on the radio before a long and lonely road trip to hear our song by Pink Floyd, "Wish You Were Here." Another thing that gives me a jolt is when the streetlights go out just as I am driving underneath them.

These stories and memories are special to me. Finding the dimes is not. Maybe its because so many people know about them. As I said, it's the events and feelings surrounding the findings that are important. To know and understand the meaning of the dimes is important. But more important, is that Ann carried them out of love and respect for those who loved her and whom she loved.

Another important story happened after the services when Angela and I went to Western Connecticut State University (W.C.S.U.) to gather Ann's belongings. She had saved every card and letter I ever sent her. After that emotional event, I helped Iris organize her room at the Romeo home. I found a gift Ann had gotten me while visiting Christine in Georgia the summer before. The gift was wrapped and addressed to me, but never delivered. It was a wooden, secret heart box key chain with a sliding cover, just big enough to hold a dime. I carried the key chain with me for a long time as a constant reminder and a feeling of safety. I would never use the special dime that was inside, the very same one from the jacket.

These stories are all over the place because it is hard for me to focus on any "one" story, when I have so many. I know I was fortunate to have such a wonderful friendship with Ann because she was so amazing. There is not any one thing about her, it was all things that made me love and appreciate her. This is why I miss her, everything about her. I am also fortunate to have our mutual friends still with me. They too, were blessed by Ann and enjoy recalling the good times we had together. This brings me to my last story, my last living memory of Ann. It was the weekend before her death, when she came to visit me at college with Colleen and Tricia. It had been many months since we had all seen each other, so we had a lot of catching up to do. We talked about our future plans, hopes and dreams. We had such a great time together, little did we know it would be our last. As I end this, I must say, if God does have a plan for us in this crazy life, I am happy that Ann, and especially our last visit with her, was part of it.

Francine

Here I sit running my fingers through a countless number of dimes, each signifying a bond with someone and something that continues to move me each day. They do not make up all of those found, but are reminders of the dimes I left in their proper places and moments in time. Writing and rethinking lets me clearly focus on an assurance that each dime holds a certain meaning to me. Although the passing of each one may seem less distinct now, I continue to hold them all close knowing each one touched my heart in a particular manner.

Reviewing and rethinking moments that have passed diffuses the power each dime has on significant times and passing. They seem to appear when I need the support, guidance and trust of someone who meant so much to me. There are times I know I am going to find a dime. Times when I feel the pain and search for the assurance of a dime. Times when a dime is a surprise, a reminder, and a way to understand that Ann Marie is near.

The summer of 1991 was important to me. I had been away from college and coping with the reality of Ann Marie's passing during school. The summer seemed easier being near the support of family members. I continued to hold on to the bond I felt with my cousin and I felt encouraged to speak about her in my everyday tone as I always had. I remember one day sitting with friends and speaking about something in the past. It seemed important for me to share, and yet draining at the same time. That day the longing for someone who meant so much was so strong that I took a walk, an ordinary walk around the neighborhood and to our local church. I went inside. I wasn't sure why I was there or what I was going to do, but I sat and stayed. There was a prayer group meeting so I sat quietly with my hands by my eyes just reliving the past and emotions that were traveling throughout my body. I stayed and stayed until I decided it was time to go. Here I was sitting in a place wondering why God had taken away someone so special to many. I walked out of that church still confused as to why I was there. I opened the door, looked down and saw at the foot of the door, a dime. The first dime I had ever experienced! I had heard of the dimes, knew others were finding comfort in finding them, but I knew deep down I hadn't. Until this day, it hadn't been time for me to find one. From that day on, the dimes have kept appearing. One day, when I felt I was ready, I placed that exact dime at the cemetery. During visits since, I continue to see the dimes others have placed there, knowing how much Ann Marie touches everyone's heart and her way of assuring us she is so very near.

My boyfriend and I were sitting in a car one spring day and discussing, for a lack of better words, things that were going on that were bothering each of us. Now, the reason for us talking doesn't seem important, although we did say things we both knew we didn't mean. We were both stubborn and neither of us was willing to take them back. We were both angry. We both didn't know what to say or do, and inside I think we both wanted our harsh words to each other to stop. But giving in was not something either of us wanted to do. Resolving it then seemed hopeless so he quickly started the car. We were ready to just go, sure we would talk later, but things weren't going anywhere. At that moment something so strong touched us both. So strong that we still can feel the impact, the surprise and the relief that we were supposed to be there for each other. Without the car moving, without one of us reaching, a dime came sliding down off the dashboard. Nothing was there before. We hadn't placed a dime there. No one had been around to do it, and we had already driven the car close to twenty minutes before. The dime was support, guidance to both of us on the importance of things and of each other. It just appeared. The moment sticks so vividly in my mind that now my husband and I recall fondly the impression of shock and receiving the support that we needed.

Time has passed; more time than I can ever believe. As always, almost every time our cousins get together, we wind up talking and talking about something that happened in the past. Childhood memories we all look back on with such reverence and gratitude to our parents who made sure we were close to each other. Recently, we sat and reminisced about games we played with each other. That evening there were a few of us bringing up the past again and confusing our mates around us while enjoying it fully. We all weren't around. In between laughs and breaking into each other's memories we would fall back on sayings we had or skits we performed. Inside I felt close, not only to cousins there, but to the memories we each seemed to share. There couldn't have been a better feeling until later on that evening, walking on my own, I noticed that in the corner of the hallway floor was a dime.

The dimes have been and I hope will continue to be an assurance that Ann Marie is with me and is involved in my life. They seem to appear for me when I need them the most. They signify an assurance I look for and a bond that will always be there. Dimes have been a part of my life through great times and difficult ones. Remembering each time doesn't seem as important as remembering why they appear and the personal effect they have on me.

Ann Marie's Friends

Pam

I met Ann Marie in college. We were roommates at W.C.S.U. We became friends instantly and spent most of our time together. We were ADPi sorority sisters, cheerleaders, orientation leaders and roommates throughout our time at Western. I will always remember Ann Marie as one of the best friends that I have ever had.

After spending two weeks trying to decide the most meaningful experience I've had with the dimes, the story developed before my eyes. Teaching fourth grade this year has been very difficult for me. I was given a very large and "needy" group of students.

Shortly after school started, I began to lose my love for teaching, and distanced myself from the students. On a particularly bad day, one of my most difficult students came out of the restroom and handed me a dime. He said, "I found this on the floor". I couldn't help but smile. The next day, another student found five dimes on the floor in the hallway. Finally, a few days later, a third student found a dime in his jacket and offered it to me.

The weekend following these events started me thinking of Ann Marie. I thought of how much she has brought to my life. I was reminded of how caring and generous she always was, and I have since tried to treat my students with the same care.

Elizabeth

Ann Marie was one of my best friends from college. I've often mentioned that I don't know what I would have done without Ann (and also, Pam Ariola) during those crazy college years. I learned a lot from both of them, especially Ann Marie. She was truly genuine and one of the nicest people I have ever been fortunate enough to meet. She really looked after me and still does.

I have found a lot of dimes over the past seven years at different times in my life. The earliest occurrence I remember was a month or two after Ann's death, I had recently gotten my first brand new car, a Nissan Sentra (it's red, it's hot, it's me). I did a lot of driving alone at that time. I had a long commute to work and considerable time to dwell on recent tragic events. I was feeling a little blue and just happened to looked towards the passenger seat when I noticed a dime sitting on it. It made me feel as if Ann Marie was right there keeping me company.

Another incident I recall distinctly is the time when Pam came out to visit me in the Hampton's during a long Fourth of July weekend (it was on a Thursday that year). Pam came up Wednesday night and it was the first time we had spent any quality time together outside of WestConn since Ann Marie died. We went out to a bar with some of my friends from home, that didn't know Ann Marie very well and never had someone close to them pass away. We started drinking (alcohol is a known depressant) and in no time at all the two of us were sitting outside the bar crying hysterically. Meanwhile, my other friends did totally not understand what was going on, and in between all of this, I was hanging out with the cutest guy. It was a nutty night. The next day was Friday and I had to work. I was feeling horrible I had too much to drink and too little sleep. I was exhausted, emotionally as well as physically. Being a trooper, off to work I went. The office was quiet that day; no one was really around. At about ten or eleven o'clock in the morning I started to feel sorry for myself, thinking I was the only person in the world working and I should have the day off. I stretched my arms over my head to yawn and felt something tumble down the front of my shirt. It kind of tickled. I lifted the front tail of my shirt and there sitting on my lap was a dime. It made me laugh out loud. I thought to myself, "That Ann, she is too funny. I miss her." She was playing with me, trying to cheer me up. It worked.

Now every time I see a dime I think of Ann Marie and I smile.

Christine
(Ann's sorority sister in college)

Over the years I have come to think of "dime findings" as lucky signs from heaven. Whenever I find one now, I get an instant feeling of relaxation and security knowing that someone from above is watching over me. When it first started happening I would try to figure out why. I would feel a little bit bewildered and down right freaked out. Now I just accept it and know that there is nothing to figure out, it just is.

The most unusual dime finding that I can recall is from my college years. I was working part-time at The Athlete's Foot at the Danbury Fair Mall. It was the year after Ann Marie's untimely death. I worked there for five years, all through my years at W.C.S.U. One particular night I was waiting on a married couple who were frequent customers and local runners. They were trying on and buying new running shoes. I made several trips back and forth from the stockroom. Twice on my way back on to the sales floor, a dime lay on the floor next to my footstool. The first time I picked it up put it in my pocket and continued into the back room to find the right size for the wife. On my way out of the stockroom with the shoes, another shiny dime lay staring at me from the floor at nearly the same spot as before! I checked my pocket to make sure I didn't drop it there, and sure enough, the original dime was still in my pocket. I don't know if it had anything to do with the couple I was helping, or just that certain spot on the floor, but I accepted it all as a sign of goodness and encouragement from Ann Marie.

ANN MARIE'S FAMILY

Iris

During the start of this book and throughout the gathering of all the stories, I have given a lot of thought as to what story I would write. Twice a year I take all the dimes I find and buy flowers to put on Ann Marie's grave. This past Easter I purchased a bouquet of flowers for four dollars to bring to the cemetery and paid with forty dimes found from Christmas through Easter. I usually have enough dimes to buy two bouquets a year. Almost eighty dimes!

All the dimes that I find are special to me. It seems that even my young students in school find their share. We have started to document the findings and keep all the dimes in a little dish. I would be remiss if I didn't mention the twenty or more dimes found by my students and myself in and around the hairdressing department during the past six months. I always know when they come to me and hand me a dime that they have experienced something very special.

My special dime story was a most recent finding on December 22, 1997 at 4:30 P.M. I was working in the Adult Ed office in our school and went across the hall to my department to get something in my desk. As I was putting out the light I noticed a dime between my desk and the locker room floor. I put it in the dish with all the others and documented it. I went back to the Adult Ed office, but said nothing. About an hour later our office staff was gathered around our secretary's desk. We were going to open our Christmas gifts to one another. Everyone in the office has known about the dime stories, but only Dana and Joan, two of our secretaries, had actually found any. Marty, the other supervisor, who I share my job with, gave me a present. I placed it on a desk in the center of the room that belonged to our other secretary, Cathy. My gift was the last one to be opened, so everyone was around the desk. It was a medium sized box, and as I tore off the wrapping paper and removed the top of the box, I lifted out a beautiful piece of pottery. Everyone admired it. I placed it back in the box and put the top back on. As I lifted the box to throw out the paper underneath it, sitting there under the box, but on top of the wrapping paper, was a beautiful shiny dime. I gasped and said, "Oh my God!" Everyone just stood there and looked at it. I always get emotional when I find a dime, but to find this one around so many people was a feeling I will never forget. From where Marty was sitting, he couldn't imagine what caused my reaction. He thought his wife had left the price tag on the gift. We all tried to come up with a reason as to why the dime could have been under the box. He explained that his wife had wrapped this gift as she had all the rest. Just then our head custodian, John, entered the office and I found myself telling him my dime story. I said, "Come on, follow me." I took him into my room to show him the dime I had found earlier near my desk. As we were looking at the spot where I found it, John said, "Look behind you. I think you missed one." There lay another dime, the third one of the day, all found within a two-hour period. We went back and told every one what had happened. I think Cathy summed up the feeling of Joan, Dana, Marty, John and myself. She said with emotion in her voice, "Let's consider it a "special moment."

Orlando

I have found numerous dimes since the passing of my Ann Marie, all of which bring memories of her loving smile.

Of the dimes that I have found, there are some special ones that I will never forget. The first dime came when I was about to deliver the Concord that was once Ann Marie's and Angela's to its new owner. After Ann Marie's accident we decided that Angela would keep Ann Marie's Subaru. While I was cleaning out the glove compartment I looked down and there on the floor were two dimes.

The following spring I decided to find a persistent water leak in the Subaru. The leak was in the windshield, and over a long period of time had caused the rug to become mildew. After awhile, I finally decided to remove the rug. As I was in the process of pulling back the rug, I found a dime. I said to myself, "This dime must have been here since the car was built." But the Subaru is a foreign made car! Then again, the car was Ann Marie's. I became very emotional and cried because I knew it was too much to be just a coincidence.

One of my most recent findings came when we received a notice in the mail addressed to Ann Marie to appear for jury duty. Receiving mail addressed to Ann Marie, even after seven years, is still very difficult. Even something as simple as a jury notice can prove to be too much. Trying to spare Iris the same pain I myself was feeling, I decided to call the number to find out what to do before she came home. As I was talking on the phone to the clerk, I looked down and there on the kitchen chair was a dime. I cannot tell you what emotions this brought to me. With all these emotions inside me and no one to share them with, the phone rang. Ironically, it was our dear friend Richie, the same friend who brought us home from Pennsylvania the morning that my Ann Marie died. It was comforting to share the finding of this dime with him.

Carmen

Since I was living in Roanoke, Virginia when Ann Marie passed away, I was not around during the months when the appearance of dimes to many people became more than coincidence. Although we talked about Ann Marie frequently and I had been home a couple of times, it was not a subject that came up. It was the following summer, when I was back in Waterbury that I brought up the subject of the dimes placed on Ann Marie's headstone at the cemetery. The fact that they were there was not surprising. I knew she had always carried a dime and figured that family and friends left them there as their symbol of remembrance.

Mom proceeded to tell me how the pieces of the story came together and of all the people that had found these wonderful "Hello's" from Ann Marie. I had always found dimes and other change and to that point could not remember anything special about the circumstances of a particular dime. My first reaction always was, and still is, to logically reason why or how the coin ended up where it was. Must be the engineer in me.

It is nice to reach in a pocket, look on a dresser or simply reach down to the ground and find a single, shiny dime. I smile and say my own hello to my little sister, even though I know there is no mystery to the appearance of the dime.

I have saved about a dozen dimes through the years, found in places or under circumstances where logic had to be stretched and twisted to come up with a scenario to explain it. One in particular was at the first home I owned in Roanoke. The home was thirty years old, and I was putting in a new flowerbed along a wall where grass was planted. Digging through the dirt, I found a dime. As I wiped it off and said my hello to Ann Marie, I saw that it was only ten years old.

Louise

When I first met the Romeo family in January 1995, I immediately felt the love and warmth from a family that would someday become my family.

Stories about Ann Marie and her life filled the house frequently. These stories filled my heart with love and sadness for a girl I never knew. When I first heard about the dimes, I was amazed, but not shocked. There were so many stories, the more I heard the more I learned who Ann Marie was. I guess you could say I felt like I was becoming close to her. I have always believed that our loved ones that leave us are always close by.

I knew Ann Marie was part of my life forever when Carmen and I were on our honeymoon. We took a cruise to the Caribbean and after finding our room started to unpack our suitcase. There on the bottom of the suitcase was a dime! Carmen and I looked at each other and smiled, knowing that Ann Marie will always be with us no matter where we go. It was the beginning of our marriage, and the beginning of a friendship to someone I never knew.

Christine

Ann Marie died during the most traumatic time in my life. Jack and I were married just over a year. We had moved away from home to start an Army career, first for six months in Texas, and then to Georgia for a permanent assignment. Within a month of arriving in Georgia, Jack was shipped out to Saudi Arabia for what would become the Gulf War. I was a brand new Army wife alone in a new place far away from home. My husband was going off to a strange country halfway around the world and we had no idea what the next few months would bring.

When we found out Jack was leaving, Ann Marie did not hesitate to come to Georgia to say goodbye and lend moral support. Her smiles and hugs were always so comforting, no matter how difficult the situation. We are so thankful and grateful that we both had that time with her. After she died and I returned alone to our house, I was somehow comforted by the fact that Ann Marie had been in that house with us. She knew the rooms, the yard, the neighborhood. Dimes started showing up in strange places almost immediately after the first few were found in Connecticut.

Soon after Jack arrived home from the war, we moved from that house to another one not too far away. I was troubled by the fact that we would be living in a house where Ann Marie had never been. I couldn't have any memories of her being in the rooms where I was now living. I was assured she was with us when we began finding dimes in that house as well.

Finding dimes in strange places became a regular occurrence. Each time I'd find one in a corner, on the car seat, just laying on a table, in the wash, etc., I'd whisper "Hi Ann Marie" to acknowledge that she was never very far away. At first, I began collecting all the dimes I found, but then I began to leave them where I found them, sometimes coming across them again as a special reminder. Sometimes I'd just pick them up and put them in my pocket. I kept one in the pocket of my jacket for quite a while. Every time I wore that jacket I'd stick my hand in the pocket and hold on to the dime and remember my sister.

We moved back to Texas, now with a ten-month-old baby, and spent ten months in a small apartment until we moved into a government house on post. With each move the dimes continued to show up---under beds, on the dashboard of the car. I now knew that wherever we go, Ann Marie would be with us.

Our hardest move was yet to come. Accepting an assignment in Hawaii early in 1997 also meant accepting the fact that we would now be in the Army for the long haul. By the time the assignment would be over, we'd be more than halfway to retirement. I had always held on to the possibility that we could make the decision to get out at any time and settle down closer to home. Moving to Hawaii would make that much more difficult. It also meant being halfway around the world from family and six time zones away. It was a big commitment. Although I was ready to leave Texas, I wasn't sure Hawaii was exactly where I wanted to go.

After a lot of discussing and soul searching, we made the decision to accept the assignment and continue Jack's Army career. It took a while, but by the time we were ready to make the logistical plans for the move, I was at peace with our decision. Living in such a beautiful, exciting place is an opportunity of a lifetime. The Army life really is fulfilling. Jack's job would allow him to spend more time with us (now a family of four) than he ever could before. There was no threat of deployments and no field time. My mother's words of support keep coming back to me: "I could get on a plane and go to Hawaii just as easily as I could get on one heading to Texas. It will just take a few more hours."

It took three days for the movers to pack up our belongings. They finally began wrapping our furniture and carrying items out to the truck. On that last day of moving out, the kids were in daycare and the movers took a break for lunch. I was alone in the half-empty house. I decided to try to make some order of the living room, where most of the wrapping and packing was being done. There was a lot of packaging material, debris and dust around. After I consolidated the garbage, I swept the entire floor of the now empty room. The movers returned after their lunch break and went right back to work. Suddenly, I spotted something shiny exactly in the middle of the living room floor that I had just finished sweeping. Sure enough, it was a dime. I knew Ann Marie was with me that day, but I didn't think much more of that dime than I had of most others before that.

After going to Connecticut for a full month during the holidays, it was finally time to leave for Hawaii. We were nervous and excited at the same time. The trip went very smoothly. When we arrived, we were told a house would be ready for us within a few weeks. We settled into our temporary lodging and after a few weeks were told it may be much longer until a house would be available and to start looking for off-post housing. We looked at several places and soon realized that with such a high cost of living in Hawaii, we would have to settle for a condo or apartment with much less space than we really needed. I was beginning to get discouraged when on Ash Wednesday, after returning from church with John and Megan, Jack was anxiously waiting for us to give us the good news, that a house was assigned to us and would be ready in less than a week. He couldn't wait to jump in the car and take us there.

It was around noon, and the workers who were painting and getting the house ready were just about to take their lunch break. We walked into the house, toured every room, and as I was coming down the stairs for the very first time, I noticed something shiny exactly in the middle of the empty living room floor. It was a dime.

I knew we made the right decision to come to Hawaii.

Jack

I can say that since I met Ann Marie I considered her a good friend and more than just a sister-in-law; she was a sister. When I was deployed to the Middle East in 1990, I could count on mail from three people every week, my wife, of course, my sister and Ann Marie. She would send a letter or a tape cassette, and even had her sorority sisters writing. The most important part of the day out there in the middle of the desert was mail call. Ann Marie's letters were always upbeat and made me feel better.

When I received the news of Ann Marie's death my platoon and myself were on a defensive mission, protecting a command and control center against possible terrorist attacks. It was in the middle of a driving sandstorm when my commander pulled up. We were buttoned down inside our armored personnel carriers, so he had to knock very hard to get our attention. When he informed me of Ann Marie's death it hit me hard. He took me to a phone booth about 80 miles away so I could call home. He also said he would try and get me home on emergency leave. However, at that time we did not know that the decision was made to go to war and the Army was not letting anybody go home. That was tough on me and my family, but time went on and we went to war. As the war started, tensions increased and people were getting nervous. I noticed a great change in my platoon, one of uneasiness and determination. As we prepared to cross the border into Iraq at the start of the ground campaign, I was very uneasy, but not afraid. I had a sense that everything was going to be okay that someone was watching over me. On the night of 26 February 1991, a strange incident occurred. We had made contact with the Iraqi army. They were dug in behind some berms and bunkers. As we attacked we had to climb the berms with our vehicles. This exposes the most vulnerable part of the vehicle; its underside, which is not armor protected. As we were cresting the berm, I told my driver that if we took a rocket-propelled grenade in the belly of the track we were history. This was scary. As we reached the bottom of the berm, my driver called contact of Iraqi soldiers about 100 meters in front of us. We opened fire and they began to run. As we were pursuing them my driver stopped. I was yelling at him to keep moving when he said, " Sir, look over the right side of the track!" As I did I noticed a hole in the ground about 4 feet deep and 3 feet in diameter. Leaning up against the side of the hole was a loaded rocket-propelled grenade. An enemy soldier had us in his sights with this weapon and could have easily destroyed our track and us. However, he had chosen to run. At this point I realized that someone was watching over me. Well, a few days later a cease-fire had been agreed upon, and about three weeks later I went home to a joyous reunion with my wife. I knew she had had a very rough time with me being away and the death of her sister. After a few days at home we started talking about Ann Marie, and she told me these stories about dimes. At first I was skeptical and thought this was just a way that the family was trying to overcome their grief. I mean people find dimes all the time. That evening I decided to unpack my gear. Now the Army issues everyone a duffle bag to carry their gear in, and I had mine full of stuff. While I was over in the desert I never carried any money or keys or anything like that, because there was no need. We were supplied with everything we needed. On the outside of the duffle bag there is this little pocket that I don't think anyone knows why it is there. It's so small that nothing really fits in it and nobody ever uses it, So this night as I was unpacking, this little pocket intrigued me. I couldn't imagine why it was there. I had never opened it. I pulled apart the snaps and felt inside. Something was in there. As I pulled it out I noticed it was a dime. I looked at Christine and understood that someone was watching over me during the war. Ann Marie had been in that track with me. I was now a believer in the dime stories.

Angela

In May of 1993 I graduated from Southern Connecticut State University. For the previous three years, since my sister's death, I had been finding dimes along with my family and friends. As I still do now, I got in the habit of saying, "Hi, Ann.", while I smiled and held my newfound dime up in the air.

My first cousin, John, (whose sister this book is dedicated to) along with my two girlfriends and his hometown friend decided to celebrate our graduations with a five week long backpacking trip in midsummer. We purchased airline tickets and Eurail passes in order to backpack through eleven European countries. We flew into London where we would stay for three days. I quickly realized that my American dollars and cents were not going to be used or needed.

I had found dimes frequently when I was out at night having a good time. You see, my sister and I had recently "bonded." Our childhood spats were long past, and we had a friendship, which was continually strengthening with many groups of mutual friends.

Two days later we were out at a pub drinking warm beer and I excused myself to go to the ladies room. I don't mean to get personal, but as I was sitting down my eyes gazed upon an American dime. I performed my usual ritual and kept that dime in a safe place for the next five weeks. Now I knew Ann was with me on my trip.

I found peace in the notion of believing that among all of my European experiences; Ann rafted in the glacier formed Swiss rivers, boated in the Blue Grotto in Capri, Italy and hiked to the top of St. Andrew's Seat in Scotland.

Angela (College Paper)

This additional document by Angela was written two years after Ann Marie's passing. It was written for a Death, Dying and Bereavement class in her last year of college. It was included in this book because it is one of the earliest recollections of some findings of dimes. This journal was written in October, 1992. It was found during the time that we decided to gather and print the stories for this book.

My thoughts about . . .

For this journal entry I would like to share with you the very peculiar Story of the Dimes. Two years ago my sister called my parents from somewhere between Virginia and Pennsylvania telling them that she and her friends were on their way home from the conference they attended over the weekend. Even though Ann would arrive at school, not at our parents' house, she called them anyway. This was something she was known for. Ann didn't make it back to Danbury on that stormy Sunday night. Instead she was the one of the passengers in a Ford Bronco involved in a three-car accident on an icy bridge in Scranton, Pennsylvania. Her sorority sister, Kelly, died that night, while Ann finally let go the following morning.

Here begins the story of the dimes. In the pocket of the jacket that Ann was wearing when she died, there was one dime. Her friend, Michelle, found this when she was given Ann's jacket. Since that time, many of Ann's friends and family members have been finding single dimes in very weird places. My mother was the first person to catch on to these frequent happenings. I personally find dimes often on restroom floors, inside bags, in the washing machine and various other common places. I was not one of the people who first discovered these happenings, but when I was told of them I started to become more aware of where I found common change. I wasn't totally convinced at first, but I gradually concluded through others' stories and my own findings that something was really going on. The places that I described where I found dimes are common places to find change, but in my instances I have almost always found single dimes.

My mother tells me of her stories and my dad's, a few of which I will share. One day my mother was walking in a hallway in our house when she found a dime, right in the middle. In looking at the dime she found, she noticed it was a Canadian dime. My mom then put the dime on her dresser, where later she would add it to her ever-growing collection. Later in the same day, she found another Canadian dime on the floor in another part of the house. (I can't remember exactly where.) My mom yelled to my father to come look. She made my father go look on her dresser where she put the other dime, and sure enough it was still there.

My mother also told me that when my dad was trying to fix a leak in my car (which was my sister's before she died) he had the floor all pulled up in the front seat area. While working with the problem, he found a dime deep inside the floor under layers of materials. My mom told me that he said that there was no way a dime could have been there unless it was there when the car was being built.

These happenings were very freaky to my family at first. My mom and dad used to get upset because of wondering and the sparked memories the dimes caused. I know that my mom still finds them along with other family and friends, but it's not really talked about anymore. I think everyone, including myself, has found peace with the occurrences. When I find dimes I hold them up in the air and say hello to Ann.

In fact, I feel happy when I find a dime. It tells me that my sister is looking after me, sharing in the activity that I am involved in. I also began using the dimes as a way of asking Ann questions regarding what is happening in my life. For instance, I asked her a question, and told her to send me a dime if she agreed with me.

I really don't know what this all means, or if anything like this has ever happened before. My family and friends are not crazy, this has really been happening for the past two years. I think it's kind of cool. What do you think?

Aunt Theresa

My niece Iris started collecting the "dimes" stories for this book in August 1997. It is now January of 1998 and I am finally telling mine. It is hard to put in words something as strong as the feelings one gets when the finding of a dime occurs.

I must say that my nieces are as close to me as my own children. I have watched them grow from infancy to adulthood because I was a helping hand to my sister during their growing years. They are as much a part of my life as I am to theirs.

I have found several dimes over the years. The washing machine, bathroom floor, under the refrigerator, in my pockets (dimes only) are some of the places. My latest finding happened just recently when I sat down to write at my desk. Since I am not accustomed to leaving change in this area (in any form) I was very surprised when I saw it there. I always wonder how they turn up the way they do.

I am always thankful for the "hello" from Ann Marie when I find one. My daughter Rose Ann wrote her own story about the first dime ever found in my house. My niece Ann Marie was special and we will always know that.

Aunt Brenda

I have always felt that knowing Ann Marie was to know and love a very special person. Every time I came into contact with her, she had the most dazzling smile and the ability to make you feel as though you were the only person on earth that she wanted to be with. What greater gift can you give another human being! Recently I came upon a quote that impressed me deeply. I think it relates to Ann Marie and her passing perfectly.

"Mourn not too long that she is gone, but rejoice forever that she was."

Aunt Gladys
Ann Marie Angel

Everyone knows Ann Marie is an angel in heaven. She was also an angel on earth. She had such a way about her and it reflected on everyone she came to know.

My sister and I had four children each and all so beautiful in our eyes. Although they all had their own personality, Ann Marie seemed to have a special effect on me. I have loved all my nieces and nephews as much as my own children.

Ann Marie was a happy child and her smile was so contagious. She was so easy to get along with and had so much charisma about her. One couldn't help but love her. Her death has shattered us all and has been the most painful experience for our family. It has not been easy for our family, especially my sister and Orlando. Their suffering will never be over. She not only touched our lives with her love, but also for every one who knew her. For the short time we had her in our lives, her memory will go on forever.

My dime story is as follows. It was a year after Ann Marie's death and I was at my sister's. It was November because I wanted to be there for the first anniversary mass. One night Iris was doing my hair. I had to go down to the cellar to get the hair dryer. As I bent down to pick it up, underneath it was a dime! We had been talking about the dimes that had been turning up. It was very emotional for us and we know that Ann Marie is with us much more than we realize.

Aunt Anna

It was just a few short weeks since the terrible accident when our beautiful Ann Marie was snatched from us forever. Our lives were turned upside down. It was just a few short weeks till Christmas, the time of year when everyone is in the joyous spirit.

One day, with still a heavy heart, I thought I would try to do a little Christmas shopping and tried to get into the "spirit" of the season. I went to the mall and just walked around aimlessly. After a while, and without making a single purchase, I decided to return home. As I approached the car something caught my eye---- something small, something shiny. Without hesitation I bent down and picked up a dime. Not thinking much about it, I put it in my coat pocket. It stayed in my coat pocket for quite some time. Occasionally, I would put my hand in there and just hold it and just flip it around. I just kept that single dime in my pocket.

Several weeks later when I was visiting my family, Iris mentioned the story about Michelle Richardson, one of Ann Marie's very best friends, and the dimes. I then knew my dime was special. This was the first of my dime experiences, there have been others, all very meaningful.

Cousin Rose Ann

Forty-two years is a long time to live in one place. That's how long my mother lived in her home. It was a wonderfully happy and loving place to grow up in; always filled with friends, family and lots of love. Five years after my Dad passed away, Mom decided to move on. The burden of maintaining a house at age seventy- five was just too much. She made the decision to move to Florida where she and Dad had spent time during the winter months.

I had the task of breaking up the "old homestead" and physically moving her South. It's unbelievable how much one can accumulate after forty-seven years of marriage! Also, we planned to move everything in her Chevy Lumina, so you can imagine the sorting that had to be done. A lot of sentimental things were going to Goodwill.

I am happy to say we celebrated her first Christmas (1996) in her beautiful, new villa in Port St. Lucie, Florida. She said she felt like a bride with all her new things. We decided to have a holiday get-together with some of her friends. While I was preparing for the party, I remembered that one of the few things I decided to take from the "old homestead" was her twenty-cup coffeepot. I was hoping it still worked, as she hadn't used it in several years. I removed it from its box, took off the cover to wash it out and sitting in the basket that holds the coffee was a dime! My first reaction was one of stunned silence. Then I looked up and said "We love you too and miss you."

We were blessed to have Ann Marie at the party to celebrate the new house.

Iris's Uncle John

I, Uncle John, was visiting my niece (Ann Marie's mother) and I asked her out of curiosity, "How come there's always dimes on Ann Marie's monument in the cemetery?" With a little hesitation, Iris then told me about her dime stories. This was on a Sunday morning. The next day I was in church at eight o'clock mass and, after receiving communion came back and knelt down in my pew. It was then that I noticed a dime on the seat of the pew in front of me. Coincidental or not ? Later I called Iris and told her what happened.

Iris's Aunt Harriet *(John's Wife)*

Just a note on my experience. After I had listened to Iris' and John's story of the dimes, it brought to mind how one day, long before their conversation, I was walking down the driveway with my daughter and I found a dime. At that time I remember remarking, "How come I'm always finding dimes?" I'm still wondering why. I really don't know if this is connected but-- who are we to know?

Cousin Dennis *(John and Harriet's Son)*

One of my morning workout routines involves going to the local fitness course in Lexington, Massachusetts. About midway through the course at the "step- up" station, I often think of relatives and friends while I count my repetitions. During this activity, I may even visualize pumping currents of "health vibes" out to people I know who could use a little health boost at the start of the day.... Often my parents, Aunt Theresa, Aunt Christine during times of her sickness. I've come to think of this as my "cosmic station," and when approaching it, I regularly expect to find a you-know-what lying on the ground. It's just a feeling that I get that if I were to look down, there would be a dime waiting for me.

Well, last week, not at this particular station, but at three stops earlier, I had just finished the routine for my mid-section muscles, when I straightened up and instead of just hopping up over to the running path, I looked down and there was the dime waiting for me. I almost said, "It's about time," but rather, I thought of you Iris, and had a little laugh.

I always expected to find that dime some- where on the health course, the first one since our July 4th conversation when you told me about the dime stories. I had never found one there before. Perhaps due to the association of my relatives and loved ones that I think about while on the course, the connection with a "dime" was thriving and, as it turns out, forthcoming.

Cousin Linda

It seems that when things are not going the way we want them to go or when I'm down, is when I find a dime. I can't help but smile and say "Thank you, Ann Marie." I believe it's her way of telling me things will get better, just hang in there. In July of 1991, I took a trip to Colorado with my friend, Steve, and his church group. One night we had a group meeting and the subject was about death. Being that it was only eight months after Ann Marie's death, it was very hard to hear. I sat there trying to hold back the tears and just listened. Shortly after, I was walking back to my room, and as I put the key in the lock, I just happened to look down and there was a dime! I lost it! I had a good cry and felt better afterwards.

In May 1996, my husband, Rick, and I took a road trip with some friends to Biloxi, Mississippi for a bowling tournament. I started to pack the van with our bags and bowling balls and on the floor, under the seat was a dime. Right there and then I knew we would have a safe trip.

Cousin Susanne

I have several dime stories to share, but before I do, I'd like to add a little something extra. When my cousin Ann Marie died, I was six months pregnant with my first child. Being so, I decided not to make the trip to Connecticut to attend her funeral. I can't describe how I felt not being able to go, but I am sure I made the right decision under the circumstances.

During this time my husband, Rick, and I were trying to decide on a name for a girl. I just came out and said, "I want to name her Ann Marie." I knew I needed to think about it some more and also discuss it with the family. I mentioned it to my Aunt Iris after the holidays and didn't get any negative feedback. She thought it was a beautiful gesture.

On February 26, 1992, we were blessed with a beautiful daughter named Ann Marie. As the years passed, I was hearing about everyone's dime stories. I had never found any for the longest time until the summer of 1994. My Aunt Iris was down visiting us in Florida and I had this wonderful dream.

"Family and friends were sitting at this table and Ann Marie walked up with this guy (a cute one at that!) and she hugged me. When I tell you I felt that hug, it was so real. She sat next to me and said, 'I hear you have babies.' I replied, 'Yes, a girl named after you, and a boy named Dominic.' She said, 'Like Papa' which was our great grandfather's name. Then she and her guy friend walked away hand in hand, and she looked back, smiled at me, and waved." I woke up feeling a lot of different feelings, but mostly good feelings. I finally had closure at what it was I needed to help me get through.

Ever since then, I started to find dimes. Not only me, but also my daughter, Ann Marie. At her fifth birthday party at McDonalds, we walked passed a table and on it were four dimes lined up in a row. I smiled and kept on going. Ann Marie said, "Mommy, I'll be right back." She came back with the four dimes and said to me, "Mommy, look, Ann Marie angel is at my birthday party!" She also found a dime in the sand on a field trip to the beach with her kindergarten class.

It was Christmas time last year and friends from work and I all went out to a bar. As I sat down at the bar, a dime was there. I held it all night long. I find them in the washing machine, in my purse when I'm cleaning it out, they'll be on the bottom. This past February on Ann Marie's birthday, my Aunt Iris and Uncle Orlando were down. My uncle was sitting on a chair on our back porch. Underneath that chair was a dime!

I haven't found any lately, but I'm glad I had those experiences to share with you. My last few words, I miss you "Ann Marie Angel."

Lisa *(Iris and Orlando's Godchild)*

It was Christmas of 1997. We were visiting my Godparents, Iris and Orlando Romeo. In the past I have found dimes and wondered how they appeared in such strange places. The thoughts were brief. My understanding of the dimes became apparent and full of meaning after listening to my Aunt Iris' testimonial as well as the stories of others that are close to her. But on the evening of our visit, it wasn't just the dimes that presented themselves.

My son had brought a game to my aunt's house that evening. It contained several small playing pieces and a single die. He played the game during our visit. While gathering up the toys in preparation to leave, I held the die in my hand. Someone called me over to them so I placed the die on the table in the kitchen. As we were walking out I suddenly remembered the die. I hadn't placed it in its box. Confirming the box didn't contain the die, several people began looking for it. No one found it. My aunt said, " It's here somewhere, I'll call when we find it." " No problem, it's only a die." We said our final good-byes and got into the car. I brought my mom home and watched her walk down the driveway into the garage. As I backed out of the driveway, my foot felt wedged between the gas pedal and something under the middle portion of my foot. I stopped the car, turned on the light and reached down. Grabbing the small object in my hand, I brought it closer to the light. I opened my hand and gasped! It was the die! Immediately I said aloud, " How did this get on the floor?" Thoughts and ideas flooded my head, none of which made any sense. Could I have placed it in my pocket? Maybe my pocket had a hole and it fell down my pant leg! No, maybe the kids threw it there! No, maybe it's a different die. No, on and on. Nothing made sense.

The connection was made that evening-- the ones we love who are here with us and the ones we love who have passed-- a blessed helping hand-- a blessing of remembrance.

Wondering all the way home about the unexplainable die, I couldn't wait to call my aunt and tell her about it. We hung our coats, unpacked our bag of toys and goodies. As my husband turned the light on in the living room it brightened up the staircase. He called me in from the kitchen. He just said, " Look, It's a dime!" We stared at each other with intensity and amazement. The dime, face up, was one of the shiniest I'd ever seen. I stepped closer, almost not wanting to touch it. Finally, I picked up the dime, held it tight and placed it on the shelf. This was Friday. Today is Monday and I have found three single dimes in unexplainable, uncommon places. Each dime is so shiny and has a special meaning to me. I feel connected to those I love on earth who have lost loved ones as well as those I love who have passed on, especially my Dad, Dan Maggio, who was a lifelong friend of Iris and Orlando.

FRIENDS OF IRIS AND ORLANDO

Mary Sue

I've never had the privilege to meet Ann Marie. In fact, I only know her mother through the stories of her good friend Mary. I hope someday this will change but her "dime stories" have touched my life.

Mary and I work for the same company and although we live in different states, we have developed a friendship beyond our business dealings. The last time Mary and I were together she told me about the plans for this book. She shared several dime stories and their relationship to Ann Marie. I never knew that money was considered a method of communication with the deceased. I must admit I was skeptical, but the story kept running through my mind.

A few weeks later I was home and frustrated with the challenge of communicating and guiding a fifteen-year-old. My daughter is growing into a wonderful woman, but like any teenager she can push me to the limit. This was one such night. To gather my wits I went for a walk. The walk gave me time to think out our differences and to cool off. It was such a warm evening, when I returned I decided to sit outside to have a few more minutes of solitude. As I went to sit down there was a shiny dime on the chair. There was no logical way the dime could have gotten there. I knew in an instant that this was no ordinary dime. Finding that dime was like finding a gold nugget. I knew everything was going to be fine.

I lost my brother when he was eleven. We were only two years apart in age. Growing up he was my best friend and confidante His death had a dramatic effect on my family. The void left after Ricky was gone could never be filled. Throughout my life I often asked Ricky to intercede for me as I prayed for grace, help, or guidance. I knew that Ricky had a place in heaven. I also believed he watched over my family. The dime was a sign that after all these years he is still there for us. Seeing the "dime" has a very calming effect.

I've seen several "dimes" since that night on the patio. They all appear during times of need. I'm glad that Mary shared her dime stories with me.

Dana

I work in the Adult Education office with Iris. One night she was talking about a "dime story" with Cathy, when John and I overheard and were quite confused by the conversation. That night she explained the whole story to us. Later, I experienced my own finding of a dime.

It was a busy Friday night at the mall. I was patiently waiting at the checkout counter in the shoe department. To describe the mood that night it was crowded, hot, and there were only two salespeople who were no where to be found. I was standing there waiting and waiting, when my mother excused her way through the crowd and stood beside me. She then pointed to the floor and said, " Look Dana, there's a dime. Why don't you pick it up?" And for a few short moments, everything seemed quiet.

One afternoon, Mark, Ashley and I stopped at Mark's father's house to run in and get something. As always, when Mark has to just run in and get something, it is never really quick. After about five minutes or so, Ashley started to get fussy (as most infants do.) I got into the back seat to entertain her when I noticed something on the floor behind the driver's seat. It was a shiny Mexican dime! Mark had just vacuumed the entire floor that morning and he never saw that dime there before!

Joan *(Secretary, works with Iris)*

My experience of finding a dime came shortly after Iris confided her story to me. I was in her room at Kaynor and she found a dime. She seemed to act differently to someone who just found a dime. She must have noticed my look of surprise and said that it was a long story. That's when she first told me " the story of the dimes." Soon after, I found my first dime. I immediately made the connection to Iris' story and immediately told her. It is difficult to explain but there is a certain feeling when I found the coin. Usually you find a coin, toss it in your pocket, and go on your way. I found several more dimes in the future. Once I saw Iris find a dime in the desk drawer in our Adult Ed office. I had opened that drawer several times and there was nothing in it. I had a picture of my Granddaughter Sara on my desk. As I find dimes I insert them into the bottom of the picture frame. Maybe because Sara is a "special" child and because Ann Marie was so special to her family and friends, for whatever reasons, there was a desire for placing those dimes in the frame. I truly feel special that I could be part of Iris' story.

Irene (Co-worker and lifelong Friend)

I have known Iris for almost forty years and have worked with her for ten. Iris has always shared things with me over the years and we have known one another's families. Ann Marie was always a special person and would make you feel special whenever you would meet her.

Sometime later, after Ann Marie had passed away, Iris confided her dime stories to me. She would find dimes at home and at school. I was witness to several of these findings.

Two incidents that I write about I remember distinctly. Both of them happened at a time when I would be going through an emotional low. The first one happened when I was at the washing machine. I was deep in thought trying to find a solution to a problem when I opened the top to the machine, reached in for an article of clothing and there was a bright, shiny, dime. I smiled, thinking that perhaps someone was trying to tell me that things would be okay.

I have found many dimes but this particular one was something. I was very apprehensive about an upcoming meeting that I was supposed to have with the administrators of the convalescent home where my mother is. I had been through an emotional roller coaster about the situation there and was having a cup of coffee the day before the scheduled meeting. I opened the silverware drawer to get a spoon and sitting there in the compartment where the spoons were was a dime! I had been really upset but when I saw the dime I felt better. The next day I was ready to call off the meeting because I did not feel prepared for it. I called the woman from the State Department to see if she could possibly come with me, and to my surprise she was willing to meet me that very afternoon! The meeting went well and in my favor. To this day I am sure that I had help from above. The chance of this woman finding time on such short notice was almost impossible! I will never forget that dime in the drawer!

Marie

Many years ago, John and I moved to Waterbury. I was a young bride and then became a mom. We met a wonderful family, the Romeos. My daughters Denise and Jo-ann became good friends with the Romeo children, Carmen the oldest, Christine, Ann Marie the middle child and Angela the youngest.

Our families sat together in church, attended school functions, drove the kids to the Girls Club and visited socially. Carmen even took Denise to the Senior Prom. Ann Marie was always teased because she was always so conscientious. In her pocket she always carried dimes for emergencies. The kids could always count on Ann Marie. Her dime was always ready. Time passed. Our children became young adults. Tragically, Ann Marie was killed while on a college trip. Everyone's world stood still. Our group would get together and talk about how we all missed Ann Marie.

Then it began to happen. Anytime our group would get together, dimes would start to appear. One example was when we were all together. When it was time for everyone to leave I went to get the coats on the bed. As I picked them up, there was two dimes on the bed! One time we were going to the movies and as I was getting into the car there were two dimes on the seat. On our group vacations we take walks together. I needed a tissue and in Iris' jogging suit a dime fell out of her pocket. This happens over and over again.

I am not a person who easily believes in miracles. I don't always believe what people tell me without some proof. I question all the time. In this case, because it happens so often to so many of our group, I can't help but believe!

The dimes appear to help us cope with the loss of Ann Marie. I feel she watches over us and lets us know everything is okay. It's a comfort to all of us.

Sandy

It is March 31, 1998, and I am in Honolulu, Hawaii on a "mission vacation" to "Nanny" for the twins Marie and Anna, Iris' grandchildren. Until now I have not been touched by "dimes" except by others' recollections. The evening before flying here, it happened to me.

I had been packing my suitcase in an adjacent bedroom to mine and walking back and forth to my bedroom with clothing. Finished, I returned to my bedroom to find a dime on the rug in the center of my path. I cannot truly express the feeling I had as I held it in my hand and Ann Marie instantly came to mind. I smiled and thanked God. It affirmed this was His plan.

Again yesterday, returning from shopping, a dime was on the front seat of the van that wasn't there earlier when I left. Again I smiled.

The appearance of a dime is God's way to enforce that He is our guiding force and Savior in times of distress. The dime is to comfort us. The dime is to remind us. For us specifically, it strengthens the fact that Ann Marie is with Him. It is because of our love of His son Jesus who died for us, that God is touching our lives.

In Psalm 111, "Great are the works of the Lord: They are pondered by all who delight in them."

Kathy

That horrific morning was one I will never forget, the phone call from a tearful friend relaying a message that never should have been..... We all had been friends since our first year in high school all thirteen and fourteen year olds with a mission in life, to have fun!! We married, attended each other's weddings and celebrated the births of our children, continuing a relationship that by all means almost never survives the exit from high school.

This bond was one that kept this special group of friends together for almost forty years. When Ann Marie left us that day in November, this same bond pulled us all together again, but this time to mourn her passing and try to supply comfort to her broken parents and family!! I knew her parents, siblings, grandparents, aunts, uncles and cousins, but knew nothing at this time about the "DIMES"!!!

I had to travel to Virginia almost immediately after the arrangements were made. The last thing that I knew about the accident was that it happened on I-81/I-84 interchange in Scranton, Pennsylvania. I left for my journey with a heavy heart, swollen eyes and an ache that has not yet passed!! During my return trip home, I passed an area of the highway that I just KNEW was the place where Ann Marie's accident had happened, it was not I-81, it was I-84. A powerful feeling had overcome me, and at this moment I knew I had to call my friend to see how Iris and Orlando were doing. I pulled over to the side of the road where I saw a pay phone. Searching my pocketbook for change, I only could come up with one dime and a nickel. "Now what," I thought. "I HAVE to call them." At that very moment I glanced down on the floor of my car and there lay a shiny dime. It was in a place where it never should have been, since the car had just been vacuumed and cleaned a day earlier! I used that dime to make that call! It was then that I was told of the exact location of the collision – I-84.

Several other dimes have appeared in my life, and I know what I know. Most of the ones I have found are either in that same spot in my car or on the top of my washing machine. Since I am the only one who does the laundry in this house, I am very aware of what is on top of the washing machine and what isn't! Each time I find one of Ann Marie's dimes, I realize that I need to call her mom and just say, hi. There are many dimes in my life, and all of them are in a special place. When I relayed these happenings to her mom, she then told me of the story about Ann Marie and her dimes. Thanks Ann for thinking of me and "calling" me. I am flattered.....Written with love and pride.....Kathy

(Kathy and her husband added this additional story in January 1998.)

There have been so many Instances when in the beginning; I questioned the finding of dimes over the past seven years. Not as much though as the day I "found" two dimes in just about the exact same spot. I was at the Physical Therapist office for a minor cervical adjustment. I had just removed my shoes to lie on the examining table. After the therapist had finished my treatment, I sat up and reached down to put back on my "penniless"' penny loafers. There under my shoe was a dime, and as always, a shiny dime!!! I picked it up, kissed it as I always did and said, "Okay Annie, I will call her (her mom) this evening!! I put the dime in the slot of my right shoe. Reaching down and picking up my left shoe, there was another dime just as bright, under the left loafer!!! I was taken aback, never to have found two dimes together at the same time. I wondered to my self, "Why two dimes?" After a few seconds I had to laugh, thinking that with my advancing age of fifty-four, Ann Marie must have thought that I needed a second reminder!!! It was then I thought of the date ... October 15th, another horrible day in my life that was never to be forgotten!!! Four years earlier, one of my dearest friends had also lost their warm, vibrant, dark-haired Chrissy in the same terrible manner; a car accident had claimed yet another beautiful life!! I did not understand this, but just "tucked' the other dime into my left loafer. When I got home, I decided to go next door to see Chris' parents as I always do on this day! I arrived at their door barefooted, leaving my loafers at my house, something I do quite a lot. During our conversation, my friend told me how his twin brother had just called to check on them, this sad anniversary of Chrissy's death! He told his brother that he just had found his usual "dime" in another unusual place!! I was flabbergasted and shocked... you see this is the first time I had ever heard about this reference to the dimes pertaining to Chris! I told them to hang on, I would be right back...

I ran out of the house to my own home, put the shoes on my feet and ran back. They were baffled by my behavior!!! I showed them the dimes in my shoes and relayed the story about how I found them .... I also brought with me the copy of this book that Iris had just given me to write a "dime" experience in!! We all just stared at each other and then began to cry. I now understood the reason for the two dimes today!! These two beautiful, warm, very special young women share a common thread, " Let's drop them a dime to let them know all is okay with us."

All my love to both of you, you are forever in my thoughts!! Until we meet again!!

Love, Kathy

Jeanne

It is hard to believe that it is almost eight years since Ann Marie's journey on earth ended and the dime stories began. Everyday we either hear or read a story that makes us wonder, can this be true, and if it is, "How can this happen?"

When Iris first told me about the appearance of the dimes, first to Michelle and then in her own home, I had no doubt that the stories were true. To understand my acceptance of these mysteries, you would have to understand my relationship with Iris.

My great uncle and Iris' grandfather were friends. Iris' mother and my mother knew each other in high school and through family ties became friends at an early age. We have been close friends for almost forty years. Needless to say, we have shared a great many events during all those years. There were joyous times, marriages, births and parties. There were sad times, illnesses, deaths and fires or just every day worries, but the most important component of our relationship has always been to share not just the events, but to share feelings.

I know the religious convictions and deep spiritual faith that Iris has. I know the love Iris and Orlando have for their children and how lovingly those children were raised. This love flowed right back to them and spilled over to family and friends. One example was Ann Marie always telling people she loved them. I remember many occasions when Ann Marie left the dentist office where I was employed, and running out the door late for "something" only to hear the doorbell ring seconds later and a voice hollering, "love ya."

Given all this, I believe that we do not die, but pass on to a better place. I also feel what I call a spiritual presence of some one close to me that has passed on. I knew that the dimes that were found were Ann Marie's way of letting those close to her know that she wasn't very far away. What I didn't expect was a dime experience to happen to me.

In the spring after Ann Marie's accident, Iris and Orlando joined my husband Bob and I for a quiet weekend on the Cape. We had hoped it would be at least a short escape from the horrible stress that they were under, a time to regroup. It was just that. Although the weather was cool, we spent most of the time outdoors walking along the beach or nature trails, laughing and talking and even crying a little. It was relaxing.

When we returned home and were transferring luggage from one car to Orlando's truck, Iris opened the passenger side and there on the threshold of the door was a shiny dime! I knew it wasn't there when we left because I had put something on the seat of the truck and locked the door. Even if it were there, it would have fallen when the door was opened. I always felt that it was Ann Marie's way of saying "The weekend was a good thing," and she was there.

My heart will always be heavy with the loss of this beautiful child and the pain it has caused her wonderful family.

Pat

I am pleased and very honored to share my dime story. Our families have known each other for thirty years or more. Our children went to grammar and high schools together and participated in many after school programs. Ann Marie and my daughter Gina become very good friends; they even resembled one another. Ann Marie was a bridesmaid at Gina's wedding. We were all devastated when the news reached us of Ann Marie's death.

Iris and I have shared a great deal over the years. We have had many discussions on a wide range of topics. One evening while visiting at their home, our mutual friend Mary Lou joined Iris and me. I expressed how busy we are and how sometimes the pressure and hectic pace we keep can be so overwhelming that we never find the time to relax and reflect. I mentioned how hard it has been to accept my mother's death, how much I miss her and how I could feel her presence. I said, "The feelings were so strong lately, I wish I could discuss my experiences with a more knowledgeable person."

Mary Lou told us that she had met with someone who would be able to help us understand what we were experiencing. Her name is Helen, counselor, speaker and healer. I said I was interested in meeting with her and Iris expressed her interest. Iris made an appointment to meet Helen on a day when school was not in session. (If Iris has not mentioned the fact earlier in the book, she is a teacher at Kaynor Technical High School.)

Helen answered her front door and asked us both to come in. I immediately felt quite comfortable. She asked us to sit down and began by asking us how we find out about her. We told her about our friend and she remembered meeting Mary Lou. Helen asked Iris why she came to see her. Iris began telling her about Ann Marie, her untimely death and how she felt her presence. Helen gave Iris a list of books to read and told her to meditate. She also suggested that Iris and I try to meditate together.

Helen then turned to me and asked why I came to see her. I began telling Helen how my mom felt she had lived a past life. She was sure she was of Egyptian Royalty. I told her how I could feel her presence. Helen interrupted me and said, "Your mother has a very unusual name." I said, "Yes, her name is Olympia." Helen was sitting directly across from me and Iris was to her left. Their facial expressions changed at the same time. That's when they told me what happened. The sun was shining through the window and passed through a crystal that was hanging there. At the exact moment that I said my mom's name, a rainbow appeared across my forehead. Helen turned to me and said, "Yes indeed, your mom is near and is showing us a sign of her presence."

Iris began to tell Helen her story of the finding of dimes. She listened and then began to talk to Iris about the dimes and her throat became dry. She excused herself and reached into the candy dish on the coffee table in front of us. She hesitated and said, "Ann Marie is here, as she held up the dime." We became overwhelmed with emotion.

Helen explained that she had her grandchildren over last night and how she had tidied up the table and refilled the candy dish just before we arrived. There was definitely no dime anywhere. We sat in silence, tears running down our cheeks and holding hands. Then Helen turned to Iris and handed her the dime. No words were necessary. We all rose from our seats and said our thank yous and good-byes to Helen.

We got into Iris' car and rode back to Waterbury in silence. Warm feelings of peace and tranquillity came over us. I will never forget the experience.

Marita

I was not one of the fortunate ones who knew Ann Marie in life. As a matter of fact, I think I only met her once or twice. I feel very fortunate however, to have experienced her in death. I can not tell you what I felt when she left this world, because it can't be put into words. But, I will tell you of one of the many gifts of dimes I have received.

I can't say when it started. I do remember mentioning to my husband that I began finding dimes instead of the pennies I used to find when I was cleaning up on Saturdays. Then, it was not just on Saturday that I would find dimes, but any day and, in the oddest places. They were in places where there should not have been any money.

One day I walked into the hairdressing department at Kaynor Technical School, looked down, and there was a dime. I picked it up and said, "Here is another one of these dimes. I am finding dimes everywhere." Iris questioned me and I told her I was finding dimes every time I turned around. She commented, "Not you too!" and proceeded to tell me the story of Ann Marie and her dimes. I can not begin to tell you all of the times I have found dimes. Recently I went through quite a life adjustment. I had recently retired, and we were in the process of making a permanent move to Tennessee. We were on our last day of packing. The house was empty of all our life-long treasures. I looked down at my bedroom floor and there was a dime! I picked it up and gave it a kiss. (This had become my accustomed practice.) I said, "Thank you, honey" and put it in my pocket. I kiddingly said, "I need another one for the other pocket." Looking down on the floor, I spotted another dime, picked it up and said, "Thank you honey, I'll keep it for good luck." I put the second dime in my other pocket. I would never question, I just accept.

I went to the store and, as I was going through the check out line, I needed some change. I remembered the dimes in my pockets. I reached in my back pocket. Three times, I had that dime in my fingers and it just kept falling through them like water! I put my hand in the other pocket, and three times the same thing happened. Finally, I gave the lady a dollar. I thought to myself " Okay honey, I'll keep these for good luck." I never had trouble getting money out of my back pocket before this.

My trip South was not an easy one, and not without incident. Throughout the trip I always felt my angel was with me. The dimes have not stopped and they always seem to pop up when I need a touch of love the most.

Sue's Family

On Wednesday, February 12, 1997, Iris and Orlando invited Michael Sr. over for dinner to celebrate his fiftieth birthday along with Orlando and Richie, who were celebrating their fifty-fifth and sixtieth birthdays. Of course Mary Lou and I joined them and we all had a wonderful evening together.

Some time during the evening Iris received a call from her daughter Christine in Hawaii. She was excited and wanted to share the news that they had found an apartment. More importantly, Christine wanted her parents to know that as they were leaving the apartment there was a dime on the floor in the middle of the empty living room. Iris felt comfortable enough to share her dime story with Mike. He had no knowledge of the stories prior to this evening.

A few days later when Mike went golfing, he found his first dime. At first he thought it was just a coincidence until he found his second dime that following evening. He had gone to pick up a pizza. He was absolutely certain that he only took dollar bills with him and no loose change, yet he found a dime inside our Explorer after he got home. Mike has found more dimes since that February evening.

It seems as though over the past seven years, each time Iris and I went on a field trip with the students or on an outing together, one of us would always find a dime. Dimes have been found in New York City , at proms, banquets, on buses, in airports, restrooms, on sidewalks, in restaurants, on the grass and in parking lots. The two latest dimes found were on November 7, 1997, at 6:30 A. M. in the car when Iris picked me up. We were leaving on a trip right after school to spend a few days in Port St. Lucie, Florida at "Ann's Place, A Peaceful Haven." Another one was found on November 10, 1997 when we stopped for gas in Boca Raton, during our four-day getaway.

Ann Marie will remain forever in our hearts,
Susan, Michael Sr., Michael Jr. and Marcy

Sue's Story

I first made Ann Marie's acquaintance in 1982, when Iris started working at W.F. Kaynor Technical School. She would occasionally stop at the school to see her mom, and sometimes she would have lunch with Iris, Frank and myself. She attended the annual hair shows and frequently had coffee with us after school. I remember her always being so delightful; and she had such a warm pleasant smile and you could always count on a warm-hearted hug whenever she greeted you. Ann Marie was a very special young lady.

In the spring of 1985, Iris and I played matchmaker and convinced my son, Michael Jr. that he should attend his Junior Prom. We persuaded him to ask Ann Marie to be his date. After a school function Michael took Ann Marie to Friendly's Restaurant to ask her to the prom. She graciously accepted the date. She looked so lovely the night of the prom in her purple dress. They made such a sweet couple. Michael has fond memories of his prom because of Ann Marie. He will always cherish the photos taken that evening. Ann Marie had two dimes with her the night of the prom.

When ever Ann Marie was home from college, Marcy my daughter, and Ann Marie would share breakfast together. She always had kind; encouraging words for Marcy and Ann Marie would always make her feel special. Marcy was very fond of Ann Marie.

On November 12, 1990, the day Ann Marie passed away, my mother, my husband Mike and I were in St. Lucia vacationing. As soon as Marcy received the tragic news, she immediately contacted us. We made arrangements to return home on the next flight and arrived home within twenty-four hours.

Since that day, Marcy and Michael Jr. have found their share of dimes. Until just recently, neither one of them were even aware of " the dime story."

Charlie

My name is Charlie and I would like to relate my story of how I found my dimes. I clean houses for a living. Iris and Orlando were clients as well as friends. My story begins a few weeks after Ann Marie's passing.

Iris called me to come back and clean her house. As I was going through my normal cleaning routine, I noticed something shiny on the floor. I bent down to pick it up, and noticed that it was a dime, I didn't think too much of it at the time, other than maybe someone dropped it, or it fell out of someone's pocket. I put it on the table and continued on with my work.

The next time I went to Iris' house, the same thing happened. Another dime, this time in a different spot, it was on the floor. In fact, everytime I went to clean Iris' house I would find another dime. They always appeared in unusual places. It wasn't just a case of someone dropping it out of his or her pocket. One time I found one under a book while I was dusting a bookcase. Another time there was one against the fireplace wall, leaning on its side. I would always pick them up and not think about it. That was until Iris came home early one day and we started to talk.

I asked Iris how she was doing; She started talking about Ann Marie, and her habit of carrying a dime. While listening to this, I told Iris how I was finding dimes in very strange places while cleaning. Iris started to cry and explained to me how other people were also finding dimes in unusual places.

She believes this is Ann Marie's way of letting us know she is there. Even today, I still find dimes in out-of-the-ordinary places. Now, however, I pick them up and smile, knowing my friend is with me.

Pookey (*To Ann Marie...*)

This is a short story on my feelings toward you. I will always love you and I know you are with me; always.

I have a million stories about dimes, but I think I have shared them with your mom and dad and I will let it go at that.

You were special and when you saw me with those bags of clothes, your eyes would light up. We always laughed together. Sometimes I look up at the sky and see a star that is shining so bright. I say to myself, "Ann

Marie is okay and she is with me." I will never forget that awful day that God decided it was time for you to be with him. I've had some rough times this past year; losing a very close friend (Mary) who knew you. I thought I would never heal. Your Mom was there constantly helping me. I will continue to feel your closeness through the dimes I find. I Love you and miss your smile and twinkling eyes.

Love ya, Pookey

Frank

Several friends gathered at the Romeo home upon hearing of the accident. During this time we were informed of the severity of Ann Marie's condition. Richie and I decided to leave to be with Iris and Orlando. Four hours later upon arriving at the hospital, we were told of Ann Marie's death.

Unfortunately I was one of the two friends that went on a long and sad trip to Pennsylvania seven years ago, as it turned out only to pick up Iris and Orlando. My thoughts about Ann Marie on that trip home went back to happier times.

Before I tell my story of the dimes, I have to tell you about Ann Marie, my piece of heaven on earth. When we first met, she was in high school. I helped her and her younger sister with their Algebra when they needed assistance. On several occasions, our families went on camping trips together. The most memorable thing about Ann Marie was how sincere she was and the warm feeling she radiated. When I went to the house to visit the family, she always had a hug and kiss for me. She would drop whatever she was doing to greet me. She had a smile that would warm me from head to toe. I would always tease her and say, "Are you sure I can't adopt you?" Even when she went off to college and came home for holidays, I still would get the same greeting from her.

My story about the dimes starts with a discussion Ann Marie and I had when she asked me why I had dimes in my penny loafers. I told her, " to make a call if ever I got stuck." She then told me that her mom always made sure that she always carried a dime to call home.

Since Ann Marie left us, I find dimes all the time. Most of all when I'm going on a trip, long or short, Invariably, in most cases, I found dimes in places that were cleaned just before I arrived, such as on an airplane or in a hotel room, not a nickel, penny or quarter, just always a dime.

In August, I had a dream about Ann Marie. In the dream, Ann Marie told me that we would not be finding as many dimes, because in the dream she wanted us to know that she will always be by our side and that everything for her is okay. That was in August, I did not find another dime until September, when I went to Kaynor Technical School where I worked for thirty-three years to get a haircut. The students had just finished sweeping the floor when I found a dime at my feet. The next day some friends, my wife and I went to New York to see a play. While waiting for the bus, we were all standing around and talking about the dimes. Mike, a friend of ours, said he found another two dimes and had given them to Iris, Ann Marie's mom. At that moment I spotted a bright and shiny dime behind Mike, on the ground between two cars.

For some time after the dream, the dimes ceased. During the time that I started to help edit this book. I followed my customary routine of going to Dunkin Donuts for coffees. I purchased three coffees and paid with a five-dollar bill. The clerk handed back my change. I looked down at my hand and the change consisted of twenty dimes. The clerk noticed the expression on my face and said, "I don't know why I did that." I smiled to myself and said to Ann Marie, "You must be trying to catch up."

Mary Lou

When Iris asked that I write about a dime experience I had no trouble deciding which I would choose. My family and I have a treasure chest of these wonderful findings. It is truly like having our own "special angel." Dimes have appeared when I have been at my lowest, highest, and in between periods in my life.

A few summers ago, I went to take the laundry out of my washing machine and on the cover (which I had opened and closed to put laundry in) was a dime! I smiled and felt a sense of comfort. Over the next week I found an average of four to five dimes a day. Needless to say, this started to become very disconcerting to me. One day in total frustration I said "Ann Marie, what are you trying to tell me?" Iris was in Florida at this time and I was anxious for her return so I could share this with her. When she returned I did not have to ask her what her thoughts were on this. Iris shared with me that she had just been through a very tough week. Christine and Jack were considering signing up for a tour in Germany with the Army. This was within three years of Ann Marie's death and Iris knew it would be a great void in their life. Iris also knew the family would be supportive of their decision.

I feel Ann Marie knew the family needed support. So you can see, *In God and Ann Marie, we trust.*

Mary

I have witnessed the appearance of the dimes from the very beginning. Carrying dimes started as a safety measure for our children, so that they could always be able to call home. After Ann Marie's death they became a means of communication. Their appearance defies logic, but is not questioned by our spiritual senses. Finding one leaves an imprint on our hearts.

I have been with Iris on many occasions when dimes were found. There was a time when she and I were getting ready to drive to Florida. In preparation for this trip, Iris had her car detailed by a very meticulous person. This vehicle was cleaned inside and out! We opened the trunk to load our suitcases and there was a dime lying there. We had received a message that we would have a good trip and Ann Marie would watch over us. One of many similar incidents occurred this November while I was preparing for a long weekend in Florida with Iris. This was the weekend before the anniversary of Ann Marie's accident, which was always a difficult time for her family. I had washed a small load of laundry that morning. It consisted of lingerie and pajamas. Nothing with pockets where money would be kept. As I removed these items from the washing machine, a shiny dime greeted me from the bottom of the washer. It was as if Ann Marie told me to be with her mom that weekend. I carried that dime in my pockets during my entire visit.

The Romeo Florida house is very special. There is a rule that no angry words are ever to be spoken in that house. There is a plaque over the door that reads, "Ann's Place, A Peaceful Haven." Whenever Iris and I would be in the Florida house, there would always be at least one dime to greet us on each visit. We once moved a desk; there was a dime under it. We would find one in the middle of a room, where there was none previously. We don't find pennies, nickels or quarters, just dimes. We stopped questioning this phenomenon and feel Ann Marie's spirit.

As with the dime I found prior to my Florida visit, I have many dimes and many stories. I keep them in a crystal dish on my bureau. When they fill the dish, I put them in a velvet pouch. In every instance of finding these dimes, I know the dimes just appeared. Sometimes they would bring tears to my eyes to think that we would not see Ann Marie again. Sometimes they would tell me that an angel was looking over my shoulder.

My favorite dime story is an "angel" dime story. I was diagnosed with breast cancer. After having surgery, I slept in the spare room in my home. I was experiencing difficulties sleeping because of the discomforts associated with my surgery. Following surgery, my next steps would be chemotherapy, then radiation treatments. I tried to be fearless and brave to get myself through my future ordeals, but the truth was I couldn't help but be terrified. There is a small night table next to the bed in this spare room. No one had any reason to be near the table or put anything on it. I never put my purse there. The night before my first chemotherapy session, January

5, 1995, I prepared for bed, not knowing what the next day would bring. There, on that nightstand beside my bed, was a dime from Ann Marie, my angel. She was sending me a message, telling me she was looking out for me, and that everything would be okay. I endured those times with a strong sense of love and prayers said on my behalf, from my family, friends and Ann Marie.

In closing, I mentioned that I keep some of these very special dimes aside. Last fall, I was driving my daughter and twin granddaughters to Boston. I felt very apprehensive prior to starting this two-hour trip. This was due to the tremendous responsibility I felt for the safety of the girls. Although I drive regularly, this was the first time I would be carrying such precious cargo on a long drive. The babies were only a few months old. Finally, I thought to take a "special dime" to keep us safe. It eased my mind to know that Ann Marie would look out for us. She did. We had a wonderful day. I am keeping some of my special dimes for such occasions. Some people wear an angel on their shoulder, I carry a dime.

Julie Ann

It didn't take me that long to read all of the stories in this book. Once I started to read, I was unaware of the time passing me by, turning each page with the curiosity and mission to find out more about this sweet angel. Before I knew it I was finished. I can recall how each one of them gave me goose bumps and how my thoughts were with the family and all of Ann Marie's friends. I did not know Ann Marie or her family, but after reading each of the stories inside this book, I felt like I had a connection somehow that will never fade.

I read the book while waiting for my daughter Sarah to finish with band practice. As we drove home I shared with her some of the parts that touched me and she commented with such empathy and sweetness. When we arrived at home, we said our hello to the dogs and my oldest son and went about the night. I am a night owl, so I usually get my second wind of the day around 10:00 pm. I grabbed my broom and started sweeping the front entryway and as I pulled away the plant a shiny dime lay at my feet. I took a deep breath and picked it up and flipped it over a couple of times inspecting it thoroughly. The shiniest dime I had ever seen. I said right out loud, I am thinking of you too Ann Marie. I found three more in the next day or so and I have special place I put them and I know in my heart I will find more. What a treasure this young lady was and still is as an angel.

I finally had a chance to meet this angel's parents and they are truly the cream of the crop. I know that Ann Marie is dancing in the clouds and looking down on all of us with a kind smile and wishing us all health and happiness.

ANOTHER FAMILY'S PAIN

The last two entries in this collection of stories are from members of Christa Grenier's family. Christa died in a tragic accident also at the age of twenty-one. Our families share a common bond because of these tragedies and we believe our daughters share a life together in heaven above.

Lindsay

Hello, my name is Lindsay and I am the sister of Christa who passed away almost two and a half years ago. It was such a tragedy for my family, me and many of her beloved friends. All I remember is that I had slept over my friend's house. My brother Jason picked me up at 6:00 o'clock in the morning. I got in his car and asked what was wrong, but he just put his hand on my shoulder and tried to smile. As we drove down our street, I recall seeing many cars lined up and many people standing outside and inside of my house. When I saw this, my heart stopped and I didn't even want to imagine what was going to happen next. As I was walking to my front door, I remember gazing into my grampa's eyes and seeing fear and sadness in them. When I got to my mom, looking very pale and eyes that were bloodshot, I knew from that point on that something horrible happened. At first I thought my gramma died because she was not there. But then I heard her come out of the bathroom and it sounded like she was laughing. I thought it was a joke, but my mom showed me Chrissy's picture that she was holding close to her heart. Just then I screamed and tried to tell myself this isn't real, but it was. I was getting sicker and sicker realizing my sister, my best friend, who I adored and looked up to, is now no longer here. I questioned God why he did this. How come? I then realized that it must have been for a good reason and no matter what she's always with us. My Auntie Pam picked me up that day and tried to calm me down. As I was lying in her bed, I fell into a deep sleep and dreamt about my sister being there with me and telling me everything would be all right. It was not long after that my mom told me of her wonderful friend Iris. I finally got my chance to meet her. She told me about the incident with her daughter and also told my mom and me what the friendship symbol was----- a dime to show and represent their friendship. A few days later I remember skipping across the street to my neighbor's house. The next thing I heard was something delicately falling. I suddenly turned around and all that was there was a dime, it shined so brightly it looked as if I was staring at the sun. I picked it up and showed my mom. We were crying and hugging.

I often find dimes, some times for no particular reason. Other times, when I feel sad or depressed, there is always that dime. I'm not looking for it, but I know it's her way of saying to me, "We're sisters, we're sisters again." It comforts me to know she is with someone her age, the bond never broken.

My Poppy was very sick with cancer and we were with him at the convalescent home during the last week of his life. We were spending as much time with him as we could. Although this was very hard, I was grateful to have the time to say everything I wanted to. He was always reaching as if he was seeing someone or something. My mom asked the nurses who also believed that these hospice patients were being met. My mom had given my brother and I a dollar to get juice in the machine. Michael was sitting behind us as my mom was rubbing his head. As he was reaching out I was asking, "Pop, do you see Christa?" I cried it out three times with my mom as my hands held down the hospital bed bars. From nowhere we saw a dime drop to the floor, not knowing how it could have fallen. I grabbed my mom as we started to cry, "Christa is here and he sees her." My mom looked up to see my brother's face. She asked what was wrong and he said, "Mom, I got two dimes back from the juice machine and set them on the side of the chair. One fell off." My mom started to think that juice was eighty-five cents, why did he get two dimes back? We all held each other knowing it was her way to let us know she was here.

Although I miss her with all of my heart, I know she's there with her love shining down on me. Life is so different now, but some things in our lives have changed for the better.

Jan

My first recollection of knowing Iris Romeo was when my friend and neighbor announced their son's engagement to one of Iris's daughters. I was invited to attend the bridal shower, and what stood out was a mother with a very big and happy family. Of course as parents that is what we strive for, our family was also large.

One day while visiting with my neighbor I was told of Ann Marie's tragic death. I remember feeling, "How does a family get through that?" Of course I couldn't begin to know how a family now changed forever would survive. A few days later I was going to do some shopping, when I was held up by the longest funeral procession I had ever seen. It was the funeral for Ann Marie. My heart ached again for that family losing a gift from God, something so precious. Once in a while Ann Marie would enter my thoughts and I would pray for the family. Of course I was never able to even imagine how it would be to lose a child.

A parent's worst nightmare occurred on August 12, 1995, five years after Ann Marie. My daughter Christa died three days after her twenty-first birthday in a tragic motorcycle accident. We were awakened at 6:00 AM that Saturday morning to the faces of two police officers telling us our precious daughter was thrown six feet into the air in a wooded area. This area was out of drivers passing, and Christa hit a tree and died instantly of blunt trauma. Our lives now changed. And all of our dreams were shattered.

To tell a little of my family, Christa was the oldest of four children. She also had an older sister who we adopted. The three older children were delighted when ten years after my third child; I was now having a baby daughter. The family didn't stop growing. Fifteen months later I had a fifth child. The differences in age made us a close family. The younger ones looked up to the older ones. Christa would take care of the little ones as if they were her own. Dressing them, loving them and as they got older always taking them to the movies, shopping and lunch. Christa worked for our family business while attending college. Lindsay would call her four or five times a day to see what her plans were and if she were included. Christa always had time for all of us. I feel blessed to have had my loving daughter, even if it was for a short time.

Each and every one of us grieved so deeply and as their mother, I hurt not only for myself, but felt the deep emptiness for everyone. Yes, we were a family shattered, searching for a way to continue life.

A month after her death, everyone continues on, and now we wonder what to do. We were depressed, hurt deeply, felt as if no one could ever understand, and didn't want them to. I hurt so deeply for my children and then the problems started. Anger was what my sons felt, as well as my husband. We all lost a part of ourselves and we didn't know how we would ever put our lives together again. We counseled and counseled. Lindsey started a nervous tick where she could not control a constant blinking. I just prayed, not knowing how we would ever get through this.

About four months after her death I was sitting on my sun porch just trying to survive. I believe in God and all his promises, but wondered, "Why me? Why my beautiful daughter, not even a good-bye." I was going through our mail, still receiving sympathy cards. I opened one from my neighbor with prayers, letting me know she was always thinking of our family. It hit me, "Iris! I'll call my neighbor and ask her to have Iris call me. Would she would be interested in talking to me?" Iris did call shortly after that day. We planned a time to sit and talk. I was thinking, "She is still living, still functioning. I need to know how." She arranged to pick me up. As we sat in the car talking with our coffee, she told her story and cried as if it had happened yesterday. I knew then this is a pain you never get over, you just learn how to live with it.

She shared a lot of the details with me, and also the deep way you grieve. All of the things that I thought weren't normal, were. Someone else had also been there. I already knew this pain; a part of my heart would always be broken. She brought me home and left me with a tape, sharing the story of the dimes and what they meant. She also mentioned that a love as deep as ours will never die and how she knew her daughter was with her and always would be. I also had a few experiences that I knew was Christa letting me know she was with me. I felt a deep bond and a connection that was brought together through our daughters.

The next day proved to be as hard as usual. I decided to take a hot bath, where I proceeded to cry and pray. That's when the thought of Ann Marie and the dimes came to my mind. I just felt that Ann Marie and Christa were together and prayed they would leave me a sign. I looked all day, not finding a dime.

The next morning I went downstairs where Christa's bedroom door was. The door was closed and, as usual, I was hoping to hear her voice, a blow dryer, anything. Everyone in the family had stopped going down there; it was still too painful. I saw something odd by the front of her closed door. It was a dime. I cried so deeply knowing that this was their way of letting me know they were there.

I've saved my dimes in an angel box for about two years and there are about one hundred. At first, I always found them in front of Christa's door. I then began to share my story with my husband. Lindsay had already known. All three of us began to find dimes in the strangest places. We always shared the story and would weep knowing Christa was with Ann Marie and wouldn't leave us. When I would find a dime that amazed me, like the one in front of Christa's picture; Iris would call and say, "You were on my mind."

I've shared this story with a few people. They too began to find dimes and were amazed at the places they began to find them. They knew Christa and wanted to share their stories with me. These findings would always be at my lowest times.

My most recent experience was this past Christmas, 1997. Holidays are so very so very hard for all of us, but Christa always finds a way to let us know she's here. As usual, we opened presents and went through the formalities. I was taking a shower knowing I would be preparing dinner soon.

I was thinking, "How unreal a second Christmas without her." I went into my room and was about to sit at my vanity when I noticed a shiny dime. There it was, plain as day on my empty vanity. I picked it up and held it close. Christa was reminding me she was here on this very hard day. I ran downstairs to find my husband. The deep longing he felt showed in his eyes. I told him about the dime. We held each other as we knew it was sent from two beautiful angels in Heaven. The day went on as usual. Around 5:00 P.M. my husband came to me with his hand held open, and in his palm was a shiny dime. With tears in his eyes he said, " I found it on the side of my chair." He wanted me to know he had found one also.

I believe that God has brought Iris and I together through our daughters for a reason. Our daughters are watching and guiding us from above and we feel a purpose in sharing this with others. We share our stories so that others will know that they are not alone, and in time we will be reunited again.

END

The collection of stories you have read throughout this book were not easy for any of us to write. They have been written by people from all walks of life; factory workers, high school students, school teachers, engineers, homemakers, nurses, customer service representatives, computer programmers and analysts, college faculty, secretaries, skilled trade workers, service industry workers and on and on. All have found other coins from time to time, but the finding of these dimes are different.

Each and every one of these stories has been in the hearts and minds of the authors. The writers of these stories had to dig deep inside themselves and gather the courage to share with others very personal feelings and emotions that were tucked away safely within. We can only hope that while each of the stories is personal, reading them together in one collection will enable all of us to cherish these thoughts: That we, are among the blessed, who knew and loved Ann Marie. That we were blessed to be loved by her while she was here on earth, and still is with us in her eternal resting-place.

The solace that I find when I start to feel the impact of her loss, is the belief that if she were able to have such an effect on all here on GOD'S earth, then I also believe in heaven.

Ann Marie belonged to all of us. She is our daughter, sister, relative and friend. People, who never knew her will read this collection of stories and along with us, keep her in our hearts, until the day when we will be together again.

September 2000

During the past years since the summer of 1998, I have received so many calls and requests from people who want a copy of this book. The decision to reprint was not an easy one, because this time I would be asking for a donation to cover the cost of reprinting. I could have written a whole new book with all new stories and they would still have the same meaning, simply that Ann Marie's spirit and memory are with us, years after her death.

There is a poignant story to add to this new edition. In the summer of 1999, I was in Hawaii for one of my many visits and as before, Mary (who inspired Ann Maire to carry her dimes) was with me. We were on the big island of Hawaii touring the NorthShore. We decided to go to the Parker Ranch to view the spectacular home of the founder, John Parker. It encompasses over 250,000 acres of land and is the largest family owned ranch in the United States. It was two days before Ann Marie's birthday and as always, I find myself very vulnerable. Inside the home, while viewing all the beautiful collections, I felt a presence. Not sure exactly of what it was, I mentioned my feeling to Mary and then became emotional because, I felt Ann Marie. As usual, Mary put her arms around me and gave me a hug, and we continued over to a corner of the room where there was a table. Under glass were collections of different writings that had been collected by the great grandson of John Parker, Richard Smart. It was here that I discovered the most beautiful poem I have ever read. I have used it on the last page of this book. It signifies everything this book is about.

Two days after Ann Marie's Birthday, Mary and I were going to see the USS Missouri. This famous battleship is now part of the Pearl Harbor Memorial. We had already visited the USS Arizona. The feeling one gets to view these ships is indescribable. As we came about the port side of the ship, I looked up and noticed that not only was this ship famous because the signing of the Peace Treaty for the Second World War took place here, but also because this ship was recommissioned during the Saudi War. Again, a flooding of my emotions reoccurred because of that period of time in my life. My son-in-law Jack had left for the war, my daughter's death, and my mother's illness from a heart attack, all within a six-month period. I became emotional again when I looked down into a stainless steel vat that housed signal flags. These flags are various colors and are used by the servicemen to send classified information to their comrades. Down in the vat about five feet was a dime! I really couldn't beleive this, neither could Mary. I wished I had a camera with me to take a picture of it.

Two months later my sister Gladys and my friend Sandy were in Hawaii visiting Christine and her family. I asked my sister to please try and go to the USS Missouri and see if she could take a picture of the dime. She said she would. On the day that I found out she and Sandy were going, I could hardly wait for her call. Gladys said that I was driving her crazy looking for the dime. She and Sandy looked all over the deck for a flag and the dime. Just about to give up, my sister looked up, saw a flag flying overhead and looked down into the water to see a dime on a concrete landing with water all around it. They were not on the USS Missouri, they were on the USS Arizona! They found my dime, only a completely different ship!

In conclusion I leave you with the poem found earlier that week.

To Those I Love and Those Who Love Me

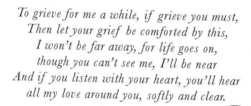

When I am gone, release me, let me go.
I have so many things to see and do.
I thank you for the love you each have shown
but now it's time I traveled on alone.

To grieve for me a while, if grieve you must,
Then let your grief be comforted by this,
I won't be far away, for life goes on,
though you can't see me, I'll be near
And if you listen with your heart, you'll hear
all my love around you, softly and clear.

My sister Gladys married Charles (Chick) Agricola on November 24, 1962 in Waterbury Connecticut. Together we raised our families in a very close relationship, surrounded by family, friends and neighbors. Both of us had one boy and three girls each all born within eight years of one another.

When word reached my sister and her family of Ann Marie's accident and passing, our families were forever bonded with love and support for one another throughout the years.

My sister's children Susanne, Theresa and Linda, along with my sister Sandi and her husband Paul, all live in Florida near one another. Four grandchildren Ann Marie (named after our Ann Marie), Domenic, Jeffrey and Jarred complete Gladys and Chick's family. We all share the loss of Chas. My niece Theresa has written the following story.

Almost seventeen years now, my cousin Ann Marie has been gone. At the time you think, "How will everyone make it through this? Nothing this bad can ever happen again." And then it did. On May 19, 2007 I lost my brother to cancer. You can't begin to describe how you feel. So many feelings come and go. Grief. That's the bigee. That's the one that wakes you up at night. The one that makes you cry suddenly when you were just laughing. Anger. This isn't fair. How could this happen to someone like him? How could something like this happen in this family again? Acceptance? Well, I suppose that comes with time.

When Ann Marie died, my aunt took comfort in the stories she heard about people finding dimes and the dimes she herself found. Ann Marie collected dimes. So, when she left us, finding a dime was, for everyone, Ann Marie saying, "I'm still with you." The ease with which this was accepted by my aunt and many others was a mystery to me. You see, I am the skeptic of the family and, yes, I would find dimes. Some of them I saved and put by Ann Marie's picture on my nightstand. Not because I believed what everyone else did, but that finding a dime made me think of the cousin I loved and lost.

Then when Chas left us, I hoped my parents would find something, even the littlest something that would bring them some comfort too. I did. I was Chas' sounding board. I was the one he counted on to keep everything held together after he was gone. I did it for him and for myself. I was glad to have had that kind of trust from him. We were close and I thought of him constantly in those first few days after he was gone. While I was getting ready for the memorial service, I took a pair of pants off the hanger and two dimes fell out of the pocket. Much to my own surprise, my first thought was, "Ann Marie and Chas are together." I immediately called my aunt and told her my story (something I had not done before). It made her day on such a bad day. I was glad I told her. Come to think of it, it made my day too.

In Loving Memory

CHARLES AGRICOLA III

In Loving Memory

To quote a phrase,
"Only the Good Die Young"
You were an unsung hero
Your song left unsung

So I sing for you today
For everyone to hear
For all those who loved you
And held you so dear

A son, brother, uncle
Cousin, nephew and friend
All these roles you played perfectly
Up until the very end

We will always ask why
And say it's not fair
That someone like you
Is no longer here

To think of you now
Brings tears to our eyes
The pain in our hearts
Is hard to disguise

But knowing how hard you tried
To be sure we will all be ok
Will make us find the strength
To live day by day

One day our memories
Will only make us smile
Although we know
It may take a while

So for now we will say
A sad farewell to you
You'll always be in hearts
In whatever we do

THERESA

CPSIA information can be obtained at www.ICGtesting.com
Printed in the USA
BVOW08s0626240716

456658BV00004B/233/P